DRUGS AND THEIR DANGERS

HEROIN AND ITS DANGERS

By Susan E. Hamen

BrightP⬥int Press

San Diego, CA

BrightPoint Press

© 2020 BrightPoint Press
An imprint of ReferencePoint Press, Inc.
Printed in the United States

For more information, contact:
BrightPoint Press
PO Box 27779
San Diego, CA 92198
www.BrightPointPress.com

LIBRARY OF CONGRESS CATALOGING-IN-PUBLICATION DATA

Name: Susan E. Hamen, author.
Title: Heroin and Its Dangers/by Susan E. Hamen.
Description: San Diego, CA: ReferencePoint Press, Inc., [2020] | Series: Drugs and Their Dangers | Audience: Grades 9 to 12 | Includes bibliographical references and index.
ISBN: 978-1-68282-707-9 (hardback)
ISBN: 978-1-68282-708-6 (ebook)
The complete Library of Congress record is available at www.loc.gov.

FACT SHEET

- Heroin is an illegal drug. It is made from morphine, which comes from the opium poppy plant.

- Heroin is highly addictive. Users can become addicted after just one or two uses.

- Heroin works like the body's natural endorphins. It connects to special receptors in the brain. They cause the user to feel a sensation of euphoria.

- Heroin can be snorted, smoked in a cigarette, or injected with a syringe.

- Heroin use causes slowed breathing and heart rate. If too much is taken, it can cause an overdose.

- People who inject heroin are at risk of other health problems. These can include collapsed veins, ulcers, hepatitis C, or HIV.

- Overcoming heroin addiction requires drug rehabilitation therapy. There, patients are helped through withdrawal with medication.

- Substance abuse, which includes heroin and other drugs, costs the United States more than $600 billion each year.

- In 2017, almost 16,000 Americans died from overdosing on heroin.

FROM PAIN PILL TO HEROIN

Caity Woods was twelve years old when she got hurt. She fell off a skateboard and broke her wrist. Her doctor gave her strong pain pills. Caity took more than the prescribed dose. She liked the way they made her feel. She quickly became addicted.

Painkillers are often prescribed for injuries.

Caity was unable to stop using the pills. But over time, it became harder to find them. Caity later started high school. She met new friends who did drugs.

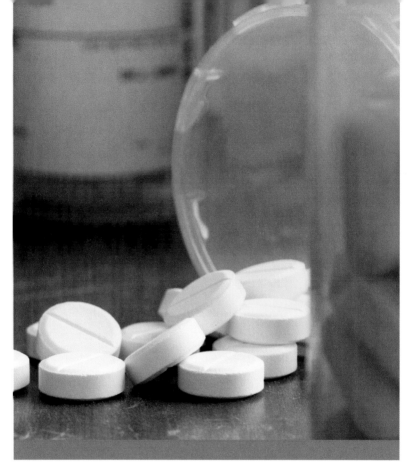

Using painkillers can eventually lead some people to use heroin.

Eventually, a friend showed her heroin. "It was like going to heaven and coming back . . . except in reality, it was like going to hell and coming back, because that one time turned into years," Caity explained.[1]

She dropped out of high school at age sixteen.

Caity ended up in a drug **rehabilitation** program twice. Both times she became sober. But both times she started using heroin again. Finally, Caity moved back home with her mother. She went through a drug treatment program.

During her **addiction**, Caity lost friends to heroin overdoses. Some of them died in her arms. Today, Caity struggles with addiction every day. But she is determined to stay sober. "I want people who are still sick and suffering [from heroin addiction] to not be afraid, and to reach out for help, and to get their lives back before it's too late."[2]

Caity's story isn't unique. Many people who use heroin start by using less-deadly drugs. Often it is painkillers. But doctors limit the number of painkillers they give patients. Users with addictions eventually turn to other drugs. Heroin is one of these options. It can be purchased illegally from drug dealers.

HEROIN ON THE RISE

About 950,000 Americans used heroin in 2016. The number of users is rising. Between 2006 and 2019, the number

Heroin often looks like a white powder.

of people who tried it for the first time

doubled. In 2017, nearly 16,000 Americans

died from heroin. Heroin use has become

an **epidemic** in the United States.

CHAPTER ONE

WHAT IS HEROIN?

Heroin is an illegal drug. It is made from morphine. Morphine is a pain medication. People who use heroin want to experience its effects. In low doses, heroin can cause feelings of intense pleasure. It can also relieve pain. It may make a person sleepy. But it can also cause confusion.

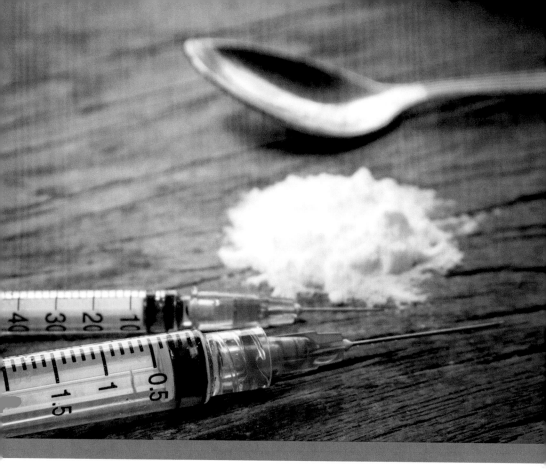

People who want the pleasurable effects of pain medication like morphine often turn to heroin.

It slows a person's breathing and heart rate.

Some people lose their appetite or vomit.

Every heroin user risks overdosing.

An overdose happens when the body is

Heroin comes from harvesting sap from the poppy plant.

overwhelmed by something toxic. It can

lead to serious harm or death. No amount

of heroin is safe to take. The drug is toxic

and dangerous. It is addictive too. Once a

person starts using heroin, it can be hard to stop.

FROM OPIUM TO HEROIN

Morphine comes from the seed pod of opium poppy plants. Any product made from the poppy is called an **opiate**. Opium poppies grow in Southeast and Southwest Asia. They are found in Mexico and Colombia, too. It takes poppies about ninety days to grow. They grow brightly colored petals. The petals fall away and leave behind a large green pod. Inside the pod is a milky, sap-like substance. This is opium. Farmers remove the opium from

POPPY SEEDS

The poppy flower also produces small seeds. They are used in cooking and baking. Eating poppy seeds is perfectly safe. In rare cases, eating poppy seeds can register on a drug test. Dr. Lewis Nelson says, "If you want to prove it's poppy seeds vs. morphine, it's really hard." It is best to avoid poppy seeds before any drug tests.

Quoted in Rachael Rettner, "How Does a Poppy Seed Bagel Trigger a Positive Drug Test," Live Science, August 9, 2018. www.livescience.com.

the pod. It can be used to make different medicines. It is also used to create heroin.

Opium sap is cut from the pod. It turns brown and sticky. Farmers pack it into bricks or balls. The opium is placed in boiling water. A mineral called lime is added. A white substance rises to the top. This is morphine. The morphine is skimmed off the top. Then it is processed into brown paste. To create heroin, more steps are needed. The morphine is mixed with chemicals and boiled. Most of these chemicals are very harmful. The final result is a fluffy, white powder. This is heroin.

The heroin is packaged and shipped. It is sold illegally to drug distributors and dealers. Dealers then sell it to heroin users. But it is often cut, or mixed, with another substance. This makes the heroin go

Distributors sometimes find new ways to transport drugs to dealers. Drones, small aircraft, and tunnels have all been used.

further. Dealers can make more money from

their heroin this way. Heroin may be mixed

with sugar, flour, or powdered Tylenol.

Sometimes deadly drugs are added. Even

pure heroin damages the body and can

kill users. Adding things can make it even more dangerous. Users don't know what is really in the heroin they are using.

THE HISTORY OF HEROIN

Opium and heroin have a long history. Records from 3400 BCE mention opium growth in lower Mesopotamia. This region is in modern Iraq. Ancient Sumerians called opium the joy plant. They introduced it to the Assyrians. The Egyptians soon discovered its effects too. Opium spread until it reached China. Trade and travel brought opium to people all over the world. In the 1870s, English researcher

Wounded soldiers in the US Civil War often were given opium for pain.

C. R. Wright studied opium. He discovered how to turn it into heroin.

In the years following the American Civil War (1861–1865), use of morphine and other opiates increased. Many soldiers suffered wounds from the war. Some of them turned

ANCIENT USES FOR OPIUM

The Greek doctor Hippocrates lived in the 400s BCE. He is known as "the father of medicine." Hippocrates used opium to treat a number of illnesses. He wrote in his notes that opium was useful for treating pain. In China, Xu Boling wrote that "its price equals that of gold."

Quoted in Lecia Bushak,
"Civilization's Painkiller: A Brief History of Opioids,"
Newsweek, August 7, 2016. www.newsweek.com

In the nineteenth century, laudanum was a popular drug in the United States that contained opium.

to morphine to help relieve the pain. The

number of morphine users rose sharply.

Many of the soldiers became addicted

to opiates. Professor David T. Courtwright says, "In the 19th century, when a physician decided to recommend or prescribe an opiate for a patient, the physician did not have a lot of alternatives."[3] The use of opiates has continued to increase over the last century. Currently, there are millions of people around the world who have addictions to heroin. Addiction can be very hard to overcome.

CHAPTER TWO

HOW DOES HEROIN AFFECT THE BODY?

H eroin can be taken in different ways. Some users snort the powder. It can also be smoked in a pipe or a cigarette. Many heroin users inject the drug with a needle.

When heroin is smoked or injected, the user feels the effects almost immediately.

Heroin users feel high fastest when they inject the drug with a needle.

Injecting it causes the strongest effects.

Pleasant feelings wash over the user within

about eight seconds.

HEROIN'S EFFECT ON THE BRAIN

The human brain is made up of cells called neurons. These neurons have **receptors** on their surfaces. These are places where chemicals can bind. When chemicals bind to receptors, they affect how the brain works. This changes how the person feels.

The body produces natural opioids called endorphins. An opioid is anything that acts upon the opioid receptors in the brain. Opioids can be endorphins or synthetic drugs. When the body is in pain, endorphins are released. They bind to the brain's opiate receptors. The result is a relief

The body makes endorphins to deal with stress or pain. Endorphins are also made during exercise.

from pain. The person feels better. The

endorphins can make a person feel a rush.

This rush is natural. It is good for the body.

It happens when a person gets hurt. It can

happen other times too. It happens when

a person is exercising. Women who are in

labor may feel it too.

When heroin enters the body, it travels to

the brain. There, it is turned into morphine.

It connects to the brain's opioid receptors.

These receptors normally receive the body's

ENDORPHIN RUSH

Many things can cause an endorphin rush. Runners often experience what is called a runner's high. Hot peppers, laughing, and dancing can cause this rush too. Endorphins decrease pain. They also reduce anxiety. They can help a person sleep. There are more than twenty types of endorphins. Beta-endorphins are stronger than morphine.

natural opioids. Heroin tricks the receptors. The heroin opioids look like endorphins. The receptors think the opioids are the natural ones made by the body. The receptors send out signals to activate nerve cells throughout the body.

Pain is blocked. Breathing slows. The user experiences a rush of **euphoria**. Other effects include drowsiness and the feeling of spreading warmth. Arms and legs can feel heavy. Thinking becomes hazy. These effects can last for hours. Drug users call this feeling a high.

Taking heroin is hard on the user's body.

AFTER THE HIGH

After the rush, heroin users may experience

itching. They may feel sick and throw

up. Nausea and vomiting are common.

Drowsiness can last for several hours.

Breathing and heart rate continue to be slower than normal. If breathing becomes too slow, the user cannot get enough oxygen. This can lead to brain damage. If too much heroin is taken, the lungs or heart can stop. This is an overdose. Without immediate medical help, the user will die.

MEDICAL CONSEQUENCES

Heroin is never safe to take. Even in its purest form, heroin can damage the body's organs and cause death. Many times, heroin is mixed with other ingredients. These ingredients can cause more damage to the body. Some parts do not dissolve and can clog blood vessels. This can cause infections. Cells in nearby organs can die.

Over time, repeated use of heroin can change the brain. Studies show that heroin can damage brain tissue. When this happens, a person's ability to control their behavior and make decisions is affected. These changes to the brain can be very

INJECTING HEROIN

In order to inject heroin, users must cook the powder. They combine it with water and heat the mixture. The heroin dissolves. The liquid is then drawn into a syringe. The liquid may contain bacteria. It is then injected into the body.

difficult to reverse. Heroin use can also cause inflammation of the brain. This can cause symptoms similar to dementia. These include forgetfulness and confusion. A person may also get angry easily and have difficulty moving.

Using needles to inject heroin can also cause physical damage to the body. One of the first visual signs that a person is using heroin is needle marks on the skin. Heroin users typically reuse needles. Over time, the tip of the needle becomes dull. Reused needles are also not sterile. Dull, dirty needles leave wounds that become

Heroin addicts often have obvious track marks from using needles.

inflamed, red, bruised, or scarred. These

are called track marks.

Sometimes the blood flow in a vein is

disrupted by a needle. If this happens,

blood clots can form there. When enough of these clots form, they completely block areas in the vein. This causes scar tissue. Blood cannot flow normally. This is called a collapsed vein.

Any time a needle is inserted into the skin, there is a risk. If the needle is not sterile, it can introduce dangerous bacteria into the body. This can lead to infections in the skin and tissue. If not treated, these infections can spread. In some cases, ulcers form in the tissue around the site. Ulcers are open sores that heal very slowly. In some cases, infections or ulcers can become so bad that doctors have to remove the damaged arm.

ADDICTION

People know heroin is dangerous. Why would they continue to use it? The drug is addictive. Heroin users build up a **tolerance**. The longer they use it, the more they need to get the same high. This is because the body adapts.

Vanessa is a former user. She talked about her addiction:

The longer one takes heroin the greater one's tolerance becomes. Eventually, the little bags weren't

As users build up a tolerance, they need to buy and take more heroin to get the same high.

enough . . . and more and more was

required just to get me to work, just

to get me to sleep, just to get me

through this trauma, just to not feel

how miserable I was. . . . It's been

Addiction can control a user's life.

seventeen years this year since I

injected my last hit of heroin.[4]

Addiction is serious. It can lead to

extreme behaviors.

Abbey Zorzi talks about how heroin controlled her life:

After a week or two of using, I felt trapped and scared. I experienced a moment when I knew in my heart there was no turning back. Heroin had total control over my life, physically and mentally. Once that drug was in me, it told me what to do. I didn't take heroin; heroin took me.[5]

Withdrawal is another danger of addiction. It happens when a person stops taking a drug. Withdrawal symptoms include muscle and bone pain, diarrhea, vomiting, and inability to sleep. These symptoms often peak twenty-four to forty-eight hours after the last time the user took heroin. Because withdrawal causes a person to feel physically ill, users will seek more heroin to make themselves feel better. A user named Raj says, "It's like a time bomb. You've got twenty-four hours to get heroin, or you're going to be really sick. You wake up, and your whole life is just based around it."[6] This causes a cycle of heroin use. The result is severe damage to the body.

Withdrawal causes users to get very sick. They may take heroin again to make themselves feel better.

CHAPTER THREE

HOW DOES HEROIN AFFECT SOCIETY?

H eroin use is on the rise. The National Survey on Drug Use and Health (NSDUH) reported on heroin use in 2016. It found there were approximately 948,000 Americans using the drug. Heroin use is declining among teens. But it is increasing in people ages eighteen to twenty-five.

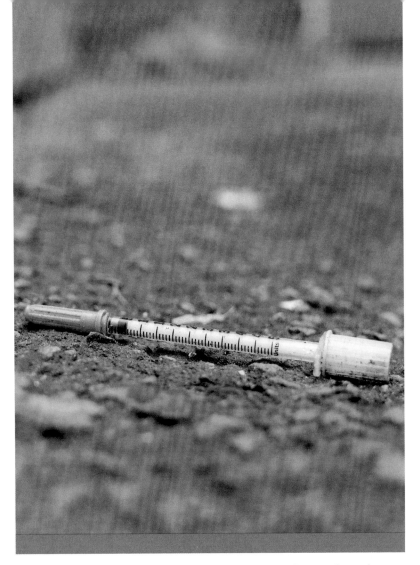

Reusing needles is very dangerous. It can lead to infection.

In 2017, the NSDUH issued another report.

It found that more than 5 million Americans

had used heroin in their lifetime.

INFECTIOUS DISEASES

Often, heroin users share needles. They inject the drug then give the needle to another user. This is very dangerous. Used needles can spread diseases. Blood touches the needles. It carries diseases. Hepatitis C and HIV are two viruses that can be spread this way.

Hepatitis C is a virus that affects the liver. It causes inflammation. This can lead to liver damage. But many people don't know they have hepatitis C. A person with hepatitis C can remain symptom-free for a long time.

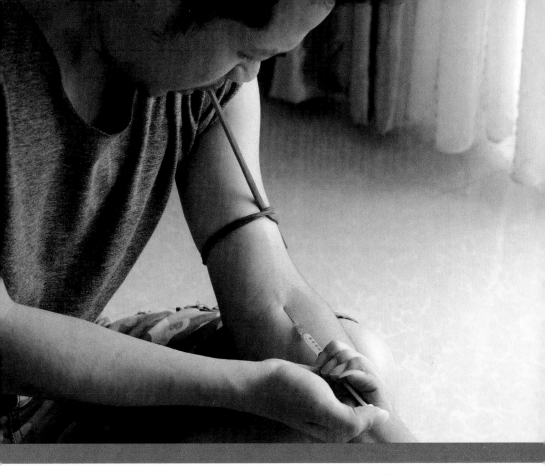

Injecting drugs can cause more problems than just the drug use.

Yet the infection can cause liver disease

over time.

In the United States, more than half of

hepatitis C is caused by injecting drugs.

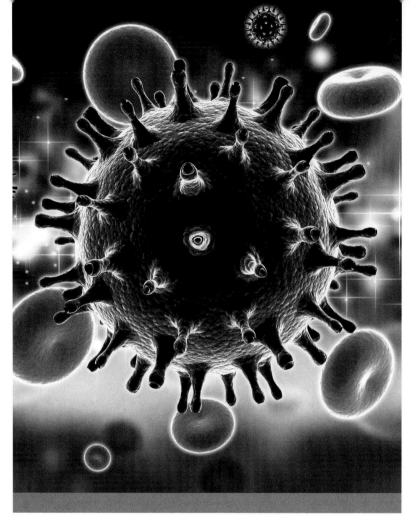

Viruses such as HIV can be spread by sharing needles to inject heroin.

Some studies show that one in every three young drug users will get it. Fortunately, treatments have improved. But hepatitis C can go unnoticed for a long time. It is a real

danger for heroin users.

HIV is a virus. It can be spread by blood.

HIV spreads when users share needles.

It transfers from one person to another.

Researchers believe sharing needles is a

leading cause of HIV infections in most of

the world.

HIV causes many health problems. There

is no cure. An advanced HIV infection is

called AIDS. AIDS damages the immune

system. The body cannot fight off diseases.

Ordinary infections can become deadly.

HEROIN HURTS RELATIONSHIPS

Heroin use affects more than the user. It affects families and friends too. Marriages and friendships suffer. The user is unable to have healthy relationships. This happens because addiction makes heroin the most important thing in a person's life. Heroin addicts become focused on the next high.

Drug users often keep their addiction secret. They may lie to friends and family. As the heroin use increases, a user becomes more private. Withdrawal can cause the user to become sick and angry. This can harm friendships and relationships.

OPIOID ORPHANS AND GRANDFAMILIES

Sometimes drug users lose custody of their children. Grandparents may become the caregivers. The term "grandfamily" has been invented. It refers to grandparents raising grandchildren.

"You start losing everything. You start losing your friends, your savings, the place you live. You lose sight of reality, your morals—everything goes down the drain. You sort of give in to it," says Graham MacIndoe.[7] He used heroin for years. Another user says, "This is not a road you want to go down."[8]

The partner of a heroin user may try to stop the drug use. The relationship can

Heroin is very addictive, and it often compels users to do things they would not normally do.

become abusive. A person addicted to

heroin may do anything to get more. For

users with children, getting more heroin can

even become more important than their

kids. When heroin users are arrested, they

often lose custody rights. Heroin use harms the entire family.

THE FINANCIAL DESTRUCTION

Heroin use can lead to serious money problems. The drug is expensive. Graham MacIndoe says, "I couldn't pay my bills, I was spending my savings, I was borrowing money from people."[9] But there are also other issues. Heroin users can have a hard time holding a job. A heroin high can make it impossible for to work for several hours.

Once the high has worn off, withdrawal can start. This makes it hard for a user to focus on work. The user may be too ill to work. This can put a user at risk of losing his or her job. Also, many employers require drug testing before they hire. This makes it difficult for users to find jobs.

Over time a user's tolerance grows. The amount of heroin needed to get high increases. A user needs to spend

THE COST OF HEROIN ADDICTION

A single dose of heroin can cost between $5 and $20. Some users spend $150 to $200 on it every day. This adds up to nearly $54,000 a year. That's close to the US average yearly household income. In order to pay for their addiction, users often sell valuables at pawn shops.

In order to pay for their addiction, some users might sell valuables at pawn shops.

more money. Users may sell their

belongings to purchase heroin. Some

steal to pay for the drug. They may even

steal from family and friends. This hurts

relationships even more.

CHAPTER FOUR

HOW IS HEROIN ADDICTION TREATED?

H eroin is a highly addictive drug. This is part of what makes it so dangerous. Once users become addicted, their bodies need heroin. When they stop using heroin, withdrawal starts. This causes very painful symptoms. They can be dangerous. Heroin users must quit carefully.

During treatment, medical staff can help users manage withdrawal.

They can go through treatment. These programs are run by health-care professionals. They are trained to help people quit safely.

Patients go through counseling and talk in support groups.

The first step is entering **detox**.

During detox, doctors and nurses

manage symptoms. They give the patient

medications. These help reduce the

withdrawal effects. This is called medically

managed withdrawal.

INPATIENT TREATMENTS

Treatment can be in an inpatient or outpatient setting. Inpatient treatment may last a few months. Users stay in a treatment facility. They receive medical care. Patients have no contact with drug users. This helps reduce the temptation to use the drug.

People in treatment go to therapy. They also join support groups. They receive counseling in these groups. Users discuss how heroin made them feel. They talk about the challenges of quitting. Many treatment programs include physical exercise. Programs teach patients to have a daily routine. Group counseling helps patients talk about their addiction. They learn to discuss their problems openly. Other patients and a counselor are supportive. This setting helps patients see the situations in which they are likely to use heroin again.

OUTPATIENT TREATMENTS

Outpatient programs are different. Patients do not stay at a treatment center. Instead, they may live at home. Some may live with a family member or friend. Support from family and friends is important. One user says, "I don't think that person realizes

Support from friends and family is very important for users in outpatient programs.

how that little bit of hope they had for you helps keep you alive."[10] Outpatient treatment is for users who cannot leave work or other responsibilities.

There are different types of outpatient programs. Some are more intense than

Groups meet to help and support patients.

others. Patients may go to meetings several days in a row. These sessions last up to six hours a day. Patients participate in group therapy. They have support groups and other activities that help them.

Programs meet at different times throughout the day. Some are in the evenings. This allows participants to go to work or school. Patients start out meeting often. They meet less frequently as they progress through recovery.

Once a person is sober, they return to everyday life. Aftercare becomes important. Many continue to meet with counseling groups. They receive help from fellow former users. They learn how to avoid situations that could pull them back into heroin use. Outpatient programs work best for people with mild or moderate symptoms.

For severe addiction, inpatient treatment works best. People with addictions and their families should choose the best option for them. Counselors can help them make this decision.

MEDICATIONS FOR DETOX

Medications can assist with detox. Some people use a prescription drug to help reduce withdrawal. The drug may also prevent heroin's effects. This is called replacement therapy. One medication is naltrexone. It blocks the opiate receptors in the brain. When a person takes naltrexone, heroin cravings are reduced. If a person

Approved medications greatly help patients during detox.

uses heroin, naltrexone prevents the person

from feeling the high.

Naltrexone is a powerful tool for

overcoming heroin addiction. It gives a

patient the opportunity to focus on recovery.

They do not need to worry about cravings.

Naltrexone can be taken as a pill or injected. It is also available as an implant. The implant is placed under the skin. It slowly releases a steady dose for two months.

Methadone is an opioid that helps with withdrawal. It is used as a replacement for heroin. It helps with the pain of withdrawal symptoms. It also blocks the high users get from heroin. Even though methadone is an opioid, it is considered safe when taken correctly. Doctors often switch pregnant users from heroin to methadone.

Lofexidine hydrochloride is used for withdrawal symptoms. It reduces stomach

NALOXONE

Naloxone has reduced heroin-related deaths. It is an opioid antagonist. This means it reverses and blocks the effects of opioids. Professionals use it on overdose victims. It restores normal breathing and heart rates. Between 1996 and 2014, it saved at least 26,500 Americans from overdoses.

cramps, muscle twitches, and insomnia. It also helps with other aches and pains that happen during detox.

DETOX FOR NEWBORNS

Drug users sometimes become pregnant. The drug is passed on to the baby. The baby will be born addicted. If the baby doesn't receive heroin, withdrawal occurs.

This is called neonatal abstinence syndrome

(NAS). It will make the baby sick. An

addicted mother says, "It's hard to watch,

as her mother, because you're helpless and

there's really nothing you can do. You are a

lot of the reason why she's going through

what she's going through."[11]

NEONATAL ABSTINENCE SYNDROME

Pregnant users can switch to methadone. If users stop taking all opioids, the withdrawals can cause a miscarriage. There is a high chance the baby will be born with NAS. The babies may spend months being weaned from opioids.

Babies born with NAS experience severe symptoms. These include fever, seizures, diarrhea, and vomiting. They can die from NAS. A baby born addicted to heroin must remain in the hospital. There, doctors and nurses treat the newborn. They give it medication. Cindy Robin is a registered nurse. She says, "It can be heartbreaking."[12]

The medication given to babies is usually morphine or methadone. It helps relieve symptoms. Over time, the medication is tapered off. Some babies must go through a special treatment process.

COMMUNITY AND GOVERNMENT INVOLVEMENT IN HEROIN REHAB

Heroin addiction harms users. But it has wider effects too. It is a national issue. The user's problems affect families and communities. Substance abuse costs the United States more than $600 billion each year. This includes health care, legal counsel, and social costs.

Drug addiction is costly to communities. In response, the government has taken steps to prevent heroin use. It also works to rehabilitate users. One of the biggest obstacles is treatment costs. The price

Drug cases cost communities a lot of money.

of treatment centers varies. Outpatient

programs can cost $5,000. Inpatient

programs can cost up to $20,000.

Police in some places have the option to send users to treatment.

Paying these costs is a challenge. It may be impossible without health insurance.

Federal, state, and local governments help fund treatment centers. This helps communities. Treatment becomes easier to afford. More people can receive it. The cost of treatment is less expensive than other alternatives. Because heroin use is illegal, some users end up in prison. One year of prison can cost the government $24,000. The cost of one year of methadone treatment is only $4,700. Treatment saves the government money. It's estimated that every dollar the government spends on treatment saves it up to seven dollars on criminal costs.

THE CONTINUED HEROIN EPIDEMIC

Although more people are using heroin, there is hope. Treatments have improved. The results have been successful. Drug education has expanded. Researchers continue to develop useful medications. These drugs help users overcome withdrawal and addiction. Heroin addiction can happen quickly. Because of this, the best advice is never to try it.

Due to improved treatment methods, users can go on to have a bright future after treatment. But it is best never to try heroin in the first place.

GLOSSARY

addiction

dependence on a substance, thing, or activity

detox

the process by which the body clears itself of drugs

epidemic

a widespread occurrence of a disease within a community

euphoria

a feeling of intense pleasure and happiness

opiate

a drug made from parts of the opium poppy

receptor

a cell that transmits a signal to a sensory nerve

rehabilitation

restoring someone to normal life through therapy

tolerance

the body's ability to get used to a drug

SOURCE NOTES

INTRODUCTION: FROM PAIN PILL TO HEROIN

1. Quoted in Mark Becker, "Watch One Woman's Personal Story of Heroin Addiction," *WSOCTV*, June 29, 2018. www.wsoctv.com.

2. Quoted in Becker, "Watch One Woman's Personal Story of Heroin Addiction."

CHAPTER ONE: WHAT IS HEROIN?

3. Quoted in Erick Trickey, "Inside the Story of America's 19th-Century Opiate Addiction," *Smithsonian Magazine*, January 4, 2018. www.smithsonianmag.com.

CHAPTER TWO: HOW DOES HEROIN AFFECT THE BODY?

4. Quoted in Ruth Spencer and Nadja Popovich, "The Mind of a Heroin Addict: The Struggle to Get Clean and Stay Sober," *Guardian*, February 11, 2014. www.theguardian.com.

5. Abbey Zorzi, "Abbey Zorzi, 22, Heroin: At a Glance," *Just Think Twice*, n.d. www.justthinktwice.gov.

6. Quoted in Shreeya Sinha, "A Visual Journey Through Addiction," *New York Times*, December 18, 2018. www.nytimes.com.

CHAPTER THREE: HOW DOES HEROIN AFFECT SOCIETY?

7. Quoted in Susan Stellin, "Coming Clean: The Photo Diary of a Heroin Addict," *Guardian*, May 3, 2014. www.theguardian.com.

8. Quoted in Jessica Ravitz, "'This Is Skid Row': What Two Current Heroin Addicts Want You to Know," *CNN*, October 27, 2017. www.cnn.com.

9. Quoted in Stellin, "Coming Clean: The Photo Diary of a Heroin Addict."

CHAPTER FOUR: HOW IS HEROIN ADDICTION TREATED?

10. Quoted in Ravitz, "'This Is Skid Row': What Two Current Heroin Addicts Want You to Know."

11. Quoted in Kristin Espeland Gourlay, "Weaning the Youngest Opioid Patients," *Atlantic*, March 28, 2016. www.theatlantic.com.

12. Quoted in Espeland Gourlay, "Weaning the Youngest Opioid Patients."

FOR FURTHER RESEARCH

BOOKS

Melissa Abramovitz, *Heroin and Prescription Opioids*. Minneapolis, MN: Abdo Publishing, 2018.

John Allen, *The Dangers of Heroin*. San Diego, CA: ReferencePoint Press, 2017.

Bethany Bryan, *Heroin, Opioid, and Painkiller Abuse*. Buffalo, NY: Rosen Publishing, 2019.

Connie Goldsmith, *Addiction and Overdose: Confronting an American Crisis*. Minneapolis, MN: Twenty-First Century Books, 2018.

INTERNET SOURCES

"Heroin," *Nemours*, May 2018. https://kidshealth.org.

"Teenage Substance Abuse Prevention," *Addiction Center*, n.d. www.addictioncenter.com.

"What Is Heroin?" *NIDA*, June 2018. www.drugabuse.gov.

WEBSITES

National Institute on Drug Abuse for Teens
https://teens.drugabuse.gov

This website has information on heroin use, its effects, and how to find help for a user.

Partnership for Drug-Free Kids
https://drugfree.org

This website includes facts about heroin use and risks along with resources for teens.

The Recovery Village
www.therecoveryvillage.com

This website gives information about the most commonly used drugs among teens and how to tell if a teen is suffering from withdrawal.

INDEX

IMAGE CREDITS

ABOUT THE AUTHOR

Susan E. Hamen has written more than thirty books on various topics for young readers. Some of these include the Wright brothers, the Civil War, and ancient Rome. She lives in Minnesota with her husband, daughter, and son. Together with her family, she loves to travel, play music, and experience new things every chance she can get.